D1709583

CAREERS IN COMPUTER TECHNOLOGY™

CAREERS IN

Online
Retailing

JASON GLASER

ROSEN
PUBLISHING
NEW YORK

Published in 2014 by The Rosen Publishing Group, Inc.
29 East 21st Street, New York, NY 10010

Library of Congress Cataloging-in-Publication Data

Glaser, Jason.
Careers in online retailing/Jason Glaser.—First Edition.
    pages cm.—(Careers in computer technology)
Includes bibliographical references and index.
ISBN 978-1-4488-9595-3 (library binding)
1. Retail trade. 2. Internet marketing. 3. Career development.
4. Internet—Vocational guidance. I. Title.
HF5429.12.G53 2013
381'.142023—dc23

                                                                        2012049017

Manufactured in the United States of America

CPSIA Compliance Information: Batch #S13YA: For further information, contact Rosen Publishing, New York, New York, at 1-800-237-9932.

Contents

Retail is among the oldest social functions of humankind. What began as simple trading and bartering has expanded into storefronts and markets where people use money to buy what they need and perhaps even what they don't need. Retailers have drawn on many academic fields, including psychology, economics, and design, to become more successful at selling to customers. Using computer technology in retail is a relatively new development. Yet as old as retail is, few things have changed it as much as the addition of computer technology has.

Through computers, smartphones, and Internet-capable devices, more and more shopping is done online instead of at traditional brick-and-mortar stores. Although the U.S. Census Bureau shows that consumers in the United States did only 4 percent of their shopping online in 2009, that still amounts to over $145 billion in sales as e-commerce, and that amount is growing.

Computer science is all about using information. In retail, much information has to do with customers: what they buy, how much they spend, and how often they shop, for instance. All of this information and more form the keys to a successful business. By understanding people's wants and needs, businesses can better serve consumers, influence them to make purchases, and keep them as loyal customers who will purchase from them again.

The rise of the Web adds a new dimension to retailing. As more people shop from their homes and smartphones, retailers must focus on their online presence as well as their brick-and-mortar stores. There can be great rewards

Increasing numbers of online shoppers are trusting retailers with their credit card or bank information, so retailers work to make their sites secure and easy to use.

for businesses that engage customers through online retailing. Online interactions allow companies to gather more information than they can in a real-world store. In addition to gathering basic data, businesses can use computer technology to find out what products customers looked at before making a decision, what customers were searching for when they began shopping, and how customers were led to their business. There is a vast amount of information to be computed.

In many ways, a family's home computer is like an entrance to the world's largest shopping mall. Nearly everything a person might want to buy can be found online, and with a few clicks and keystrokes, purchases can be secured and shipped straight to the front door. Mobile devices also grant people access to the Internet and have become another driver of e-commerce.

As ever more people turn to online retail for their shopping needs, the companies that sell to them need workers who can use computer technology efficiently and intelligently. Businesses want to make the online buying experience as easy as passing through a checkout counter. However, the amount of work needed to make that happen is greater than many people realize. E-commerce needs people who are skilled at business but also knowledgeable about computers.

The first Web page designs were done completely in a computer language called hypertext markup language, or HTML. Early Web pages emphasized function much more than design. Since then, Web page design has become more elaborate. Although HTML and similar coding exists under the surface of a page, modern software lets Web page designers see what a page looks like as they design it. Web page designers who work for online retailers need to be able to manipulate the code that runs the pages on a Web site, while also having an eye for appealing layout and style.

THE WORLD WIDE WEB

The Internet originated as an academic tool. In the 1960s, scientists and researchers saw great potential in networking a series of remote computers to share data and research. According to *A Brief History of the Internet*, an academic paper written by Barry Leiner and other Internet pioneers, a mere four computers linked together represented the birth of the Internet. Over time, more institutions, research firms, and universities connected to this growing network. Access expanded to personal computers, and individuals were able to communicate with others over this network.

Later, companies like America Online and CompuServe commercialized the Internet by selling people the means to access it through their networks. The number of citizens flocking online made it necessary to develop a visual interface that made interacting with the Internet simpler. Like other media, the Web became an important means of advertising and selling to customers. Today, many online retailers employ whole teams of people dedicated to creating a positive Web experience.

LEARNING BY DOING

Today's students are very comfortable using the Web. Most schools use Web sites for educational purposes and for communication with students. Growing up with the Internet gives young people the advantage of familiarity that previous generations did not have. Even so, knowing how to use a Web site is different from knowing how to make one.

To help students become better at working with Web technology, some high schools offer classes in which students can learn about programming or Web page design. Other high schools allow students to take such a course from a community college or vo-tech school for credit.

Students can also take it upon themselves to learn these important skills. If the school library does not have books that teach Web design, the public library probably does. Community education is another great resource that regularly offers computer classes, including ones on Web site construction. What's more, with access to the Internet, young people can find sites that teach these skills. They can also practice with the benefit of seeing the results of their work immediately.

Many Web designers are self-taught, having learned HTML and CSS (cascading style sheets) on their own. With working

High school students should take full advantage of their schools' computer classes to work on Web projects. There, they can get help and support from others if needed.

knowledge of Web design software, a beginning Web designer might be capable of doing basic Web design for smaller online retailers who simply want to have a way to inform and inter-act with customers. For transactions, the Web designer might need to install a simple shopping cart or link the retail site to a third-party payment system such as PayPal or Amazon Payments.

At larger companies, someone other than the Web designer, such as a marketing director, usually writes much of the text that appears on a retail Web site. However, a Web designer with strong writing skills is appealing to such employers because he or she might be able to generate further content for the site after its initial design.

Sites that do not change much, sometimes called static sites, might require hiring a Web designer for a one-time freelance project. The more needs a retailer has, and the more complex the site, the more likely it is that the work is shared by a team, whether it is freelancers or company employees. These team members usually have extensive training and experience.

SUCCESS STORY: "1-CLICK"

The Web development team at Amazon.com knew that many customers visited the site looking to buy one specific item and didn't intend to spend lots of time shopping. This gave Amazon's user interaction designers the idea to create a quick means of making a single purchase. The company's Web developers and designers created a button that appeared on each product's page that allowed registered members to bypass the standard shopping cart checkout experience. By clicking on the "1-Click" button, customers could pay with a credit card on file and have their purchase shipped to their home address. It was revolutionary enough that Amazon filed for a patent on the "1-Click" shopping cart system. This means that other companies must license the solution if they want to use a similar process.

WEB DEVELOPERS

People who are interested in working on the functionality of a Web site instead of its appearance may want to look into Web development. Web developers program and create the unique elements of a Web site to best showcase the retailer's products and make it possible for customers to find and purchase what they need. All the actions a retailer wants its customers to be able to perform become the responsibility of the Web developer.

Those who want to be Web developers should learn as many programming languages used in Web site creation as

Web programmers design and create the connections between bits of retail information, enabling customers to use a Web site to find the products they want.

possible. Knowing HTML and CSS is important, but a Web developer will probably use PHP, Perl, C++, Java, Visual Basic, and MySQL as well. Many sites need to connect to a database, so a Web developer needs to know how to integrate with databases or how to program for them. Retailers often want to hire someone with a bachelor's degree in computer science or Web development. Potential employers also like to see examples of previous projects and might ask a candidate to code a page to certain specifications as a test.

There are certifications available for all of the primary Web languages, and a potential Web developer would benefit from pursuing them. ASP, HTML, CSS, JavaScript, jQuery, XML, and PHP are among the most common certifications. Having certification in critical Web skills demonstrates proven ability in those areas. Completing such certifications can make it easier or more likely for a person to get hired. Some institutions offer only certification testing, which tests a person's knowledge and awards certification upon passing. Others offer certification courses, which teach or reinforce the skill in question before the candidate takes the test. Those institutions may or may not offer the certification tests as well.

Certifications are usually open to everyone and do not require any sort of degree, including a high school degree. If a person has the necessary knowledge and skill, he or she can become certified. Companies such as Microsoft and IBM offer certification services online for their systems and hardware. Many companies give the people they have certified increased access to customer service, software and hardware experts, and other help. Avoiding being put on hold is a leading benefit of certification.

WEB GRAPHIC DESIGN

Even if a company's Web site uses many photographs owned or licensed by the company, it's a safe bet that a graphic designer will need to be involved. Graphic designers concentrate on all the visual aspects of the Web site. It's common for a Web graphic designer to be involved in creating logos, images, fonts, and animations.

In addition, many Web sites embed special interactive objects, which are designed in either a program called Adobe Flash or in enhanced HTML5. These objects are popular for Web advertising and entertainment because they can handle

Using a tablet and stylus, many graphic designers save time by creating images directly on the computer.

video, audio, and animation. They can usually play in mobile browsers and on smartphones, too.

A Web graphic designer should be an artistic person who is able to draw, design, and modify images using computer programs such as Photoshop, Flash, and Illustrator. Working with digital files makes it easier to integrate these visual elements into the page design. These skills can be honed by taking online classes in Web design or by getting an associate's or bachelor's degree in Web graphic design.

USER INTERACTION DESIGNER

Few things can turn customers away from an online retailer's Web site faster than a frustrating experience. A user interaction designer is brought on board to prevent and solve these kinds of problems. By anticipating and understanding what customers hope to do on a Web site, a user interaction designer finds ways to make it simple for customers to use the site.

People who are both creative and analytical make capable user interaction designers. Knowing how to program for the Web is extremely helpful, but many user interaction designers are just as likely to map out their vision for new features on paper to share with the Web development team.

It's not always necessary to reinvent the wheel to solve Web site concerns. A user interaction designer develops knowledge of what other companies are doing and what third-party solutions exist that could be purchased or licensed for use on the Web site. A bachelor's degree in computer science or equivalent real-world experience would give a job candidate that knowledge.

INTERVIEW WITH A USER EXPERIENCE ENGINEER

Kirsten Matti's job title is Senior User Experience Engineer. Her employer, Sympoz Inc., created the Web site Craftsy.com as a hub for online learning related to arts and crafts, such as quilting and cake decorating. Matti likens her work in user experience design to frosting one of those cakes. Her job is to make the site appealing and intuitive for users to work with. Matti earned a bachelor's degree in studio arts. In her college program she learned to use Adobe's Photoshop and Illustrator programs, and studied the basics of typography and commercial design.

A good user experience engineer, Matti says, is "the kind of person who spends a lot of time at home figuring out how to make commercial products you have seen yourself because you think you could make it better or cheaper. You should also thrive in an environment that is constantly changing and enjoy constantly learning new things. An eye for detail, inquisitiveness, and persistence are great character traits for this job."

User experience is a field that continually offers new challenges. The experience must be tailored to the devices people use, and there are always new products coming out. Matti says, "The world of UX seems to be gravitating towards mobile applications. More and more people are shopping and getting their entertainment from devices like the iPhone, Android, iPad, Kindle, and similar devices. This means that we need to start thinking about how to get our designs to be adaptable and equally usable on a wide variety of platforms, screen sizes, and connection speeds. Mobile devices also seem to be replacing devices that were once ubiquitous. Instead of using a remote control, you use your iPad; instead of buying a textbook, you download it to your Kindle. Finding better ways to make everyday tools and sources of information available at your fingertips is an exciting challenge."

PROJECT MANAGERS

Everything contained within a retail Web site—from the informational pages about the company to the product descriptions to the interactive features—has a purpose. For online retailers, that purpose is to give customers enough information and ease of use to encourage a purchase. The more products and services a retailer provides, the larger

A Web design project manager must be able to communicate clearly and delegate responsibilities and tasks effectively.

and more complex its Web site tends to become. If an online retailer wants a Web site with a lot of components or needs major features added, a project manager is often needed to coordinate the effort.

Project managers oversee projects from start to finish and make sure that they meet the company's requirements. Facilitating communication between team members is a primary role of the project manager so that the work is coordinated and conforms to the company's vision. In addition, a project manager often controls the team's budget and timeline for completion. He or she must make sure the various pieces of the project are completed on time and within the budget allotted.

A Web design project manager is almost always a Web designer or developer, but one with many years of prior experience working on large projects. In addition to skills in Web design, having experience or education in business or management can be a great help in this role.

CHAPTER 2

Points of Entry

Going to a seller's Web site from a personal computer purchases is still the most common and popular way of making purchases online. In the twenty-first century, however, any device that can connect to an online network can potentially be a tool for e-commerce. Today, customers can make purchases without having to sit down at an old-fashioned terminal.

A number of mobile devices are essentially portable personal computers, sometimes called tablet PCs. These devices can do many of the things a regular computer or laptop can, and they often have Web browsers on them. Every year, mobile computing devices are getting better at displaying Web pages. Web designers often make different versions of their sites for mobile devices, although they no longer need to use a different coding method to do so.

PROGRAMMING SOFTWARE

A program tells a computer what to do, when to do it, and what to do next upon completion. Programming languages provide a way to input commands that can be converted to the binary language of 1s and 0s that a computer understands. However, these languages do not all work the same way. The more ways a person can program computers, the more valuable an employee that person is.

Web page programming can be done in any number of programs, but the code it produces still matches a set of universally accepted standards. For the most part, a page looks the same on any browser, and the source code reads the same way.

When a retailer wants a device to network to a specific location, the retailer must hire someone to create the software to do it. The person who writes this code is often called a software engineer. The programming language used usually depends upon what device the program will run on. Computers from Apple use a different operating system than other computers. Tablet PCs, smartphones, and gaming consoles also use specialized operating systems.

DIGITAL STOREFRONTS

The end goal of all online retail is to sell products and services. To help bring customers to its store, Apple's iTunes offers helpful extras such as social networking between a music artist's fans or a recommendation system to help customers find musicians they enjoy. Yet the key goal is to sell digital copies of songs, TV shows, movies, and books. It benefits Apple and other retailers to create as many entry points into the purchasing process as possible. A Web site is only one of them.

Many other programs besides Web browsers that run on home computers and consumer devices are capable of engaging in online retail. For example, storefront software programs like iTunes let people make purchases right from within the software. Entertainment apps like *Angry Birds* let customers purchase new levels from within the app. The ability to buy products, upgrades, and additional plug-ins is often a critical part of the program's features.

An engaging digital storefront, such as the iTunes Store, helps customers choose what to buy now and what they might want to buy next.

A software engineer must have good working knowledge of standard programming languages such as Java, C++, C#, and Perl. However, a software engineer might also have to learn a proprietary language for whatever hardware he or she is writing for. If the software engineer works for the company that produces the hardware, the language and programming tools are readily available. Programmers or software engineers who do not work for the company need to request a company's software development kit, or SDK. The SDK contains all the digital tools needed to create code for that company's particular platform.

SUCCESS STORY: ITUNES

At the end of the twentieth century, computer-savvy music fans and the music industry were at each other's throats. While digital files on CDs made it easy for people to store songs on computers, the Internet made it easy for people to share them with friends or even strangers. One inventive programmer, nineteen-year-old Shawn Fanning, created a file-sharing program called Napster that essentially let people have all the music they wanted without paying for it.

Apple saw an opportunity to make fans and music companies happier. The company bought some software from outside software designers and used it to create a music-playing program called iTunes. The program initially worked like a jukebox for an owner's CDs. The iTunes program became extremely popular, especially when combined with iPods, Apple's portable music players. The iPod's software had been designed to let users store and sort lots of songs easily. The iPod and other MP3 players became popular enough that Apple convinced music companies to let their artists' songs and albums be sold directly through an online store.

Today, the iTunes Store sells music, books, television shows, and movies through its online-only service. That service is accessed not just on computers, but also on portable devices and phones. The iTunes Store has served as a model and competitor for every other online music store since, including a newer, legal Napster.

MOBILE APP DEVELOPER

With the growth in popularity of smartphones and portable devices, there has also been an increase in the need for app developers. An app, which is short for application, is a specialized program that is built to run on a particular device or

Using Wi-Fi and mobile apps, customers can browse and purchase items from almost anywhere.

set of devices. The platform determines what languages or tools a software designer needs in order to create the product. Many online retailers have apps that work alongside their Web sites as a way to communicate with customers and let them make purchases or manage their accounts. For instance, a customer might be able to order a pizza, pay for it, and have it delivered by using a smartphone app from Papa John's or Domino's.

Apple's popular iPhone, iPad, and other consumer portables run on the iOS operating system. To create programs for any of these devices, a programmer must pay an annual license fee to use the company's SDK. Apple's SDK has tools and programming software to help write, test, and submit programs for distribution.

Microsoft portable devices use a combination of development tools such as Visual Basic, Silverlight, and XNA.

Learning any of these languages would help someone pre-pare to make apps for a Windows Phone.

Android is an open-source platform, meaning that the code and design are free and open to everyone for use. People who can already code in Java have most of the knowledge necessary to begin working on apps for Android devices. By joining online communities and reading tutori-als or books about Android-specific language, programmers can expand their knowledge and write for a number of different smartphones, tablet PCs, and other consumer devices. The Amazon Kindle and the Barnes & Noble Nook are two examples of devices that use the Android platform. While both devices are designed for reading e-books, they can also run apps, which can be purchased on the devices through an online store. Programmers can write programs for each by applying a proprietary add-on to Android that comes with each company's SDK.

API ANALYST

One way to make an online resource more attractive to new customers is to make a Web site, application, or device interact with popular sites or software. For example, online retailers often try to attract new customers by including a social media feature that lets users post to Facebook or Twitter whenever they make purchases. Since nearly all soft-ware uses some proprietary programming code, two pieces of software are unlikely to share directions easily. So when a company wants to make its features available to others, it releases an application programming interface (API). An

API gives programmers a way to let their software communicate with someone else's.

Many companies who share their APIs publicly or do a lot of integration with outside resources employ an API analyst. API analysts help clients work with company APIs. They might also be responsible for learning how to use the APIs of external software the company's software needs to connect with. An API analyst usually needs a bachelor's degree in computer science and a strong grasp of programming principles in order to understand what each API's commands are used for.

SOFTWARE ANALYST

Software and hardware work hand in hand, as software makes use of the hardware's capabilities in order to function. While there may be standard features in all kinds of smartphones, computers, and tablet PCs, many platforms and devices have unique features or inputs. This means that a program written for one platform probably won't work properly when run on a different platform. If online retailers can get their apps or storefront programs on multiple platforms, they expand their opportunities to reach customers.

In these cases, companies or software engineers have to port, or optimize a program, so that it can run on a different platform. Programmers who port apps need to be knowledgeable in both the original programming language and the language of the new platform. They must know how to modify the code on both platforms to get the desired results from the program without creating errors.

LEVEL-90 ELF SEEKS WORK

Massively multiplayer online games (known as MMOGs or MMOs) offer a constant game environment to which players join in and drop off at will, playing alongside thousands of others in a game that never entirely ends. Such games make money by selling premium items inside the game or through subscription fees.

Customer service for these games can literally take on a unique appearance. Game masters are a game company's employees who assist playing customers using in-game avatars. These employees do not need to have programming or computer science skills, but should be friendly, good at communicating with people, and well versed in of the game's content, mechanics, and common bugs. They have software tools that players do not that allow them to help customers who are having in-game problems. Game masters usually use a computerized ticketing system that allows them to answer, track, and then file any completed requests from customers.

FUN AND GAMES

In the early years of the Internet, only people with an expensive permanent connection could be online all the time. For most people, accessing the World Wide Web meant using a phone line to dial into a server. Since this kept the phone line from being used for anything else, people didn't tend to stay online for very long. Since data

Several companies, such as Microsoft with its Xbox 360 console, have tried to give users an all-in-one experience by integrating with popular online activities.

passed back and forth slowly, online entertainment often involved lots of text or simple graphics.

Today, permanent connections and high-speed broadband are widespread enough that entertainment consoles such as Microsoft's Xbox 360 and Sony's PlayStation 3 can be online any time they are in use. With games for the Xbox 360, at least some online element is required in any game written for the platform. Software engineers and game developers must not only program their games for a particular platform but also understand and write in network capabilities.

Console entertainment devices and handheld ones such as the Nintendo DS and Sony Vita have online stores that run directly on those machines. The manufacturers use software engineers to write and update software used for sorting through the catalog of offerings, making purchases, and downloading purchased programs.

The payoff for this extra effort is an online retail system that often allows companies to profit from their products beyond the sale price alone. Downloadable content, or DLC, is a major moneymaker for software companies and console manufacturers, who often make more profit from DLC than from retail copies of the game. Digital downloads also eliminate packaging and shipping costs, so they keep costs low for publishers.

PROGRAMMER CERTIFICATIONS

As with Web languages, there are certification opportunities for programming languages as well. Beginning programmers might become certified in such common programming environments as Microsoft Visual Studio, C, C++, Perl, and UNIX. However, most of the time, the biggest factor in getting a programming job is one's ability to code. Certification is less valuable to a programmer than experience and the ability to make elegant code that works as designed.

Online Retail
Operations

Before the customer ever reaches the Web site, app, or other point of e-commerce, hundreds of hours have gone into making the underlying structure reliable and secure. Like the wiring and plumbing of a real-world building, a lot of things must already be in place under the surface. The customer interface is only the top layer of a more complex design of systems that few customers ever think about, such as security and maintenance. A real-world store has to be organized and take precautions to avoid breakdowns or loss through theft. The digital side of retail has its own, similar problems that must be taken into consideration. The technical solutions for these problems come from another group of computer-proficient employees.

QUALITY ASSURANCE TESTER

Every new piece of software goes through a stage known as quality assurance. During this time, the software is tested thoroughly to look for bugs or errors. Quality assurance personnel are not necessarily programmers, but they are thorough and detail-oriented. They try every feature and function on the app or Web site and make specific notes about things that go wrong or need improvement.

In many cases, testers do not have a lot of knowledge about the inner workings of the software. A tester must think like a

Many game enthusiasts imagine that testing games would be a dream job. In reality, quality assurance testers put in long hours performing repetitive tasks and documenting bugs.

customer and try to do things a customer might do. Knowing too much about how everything works can keep a tester from thinking of the unexpected things that a new user will sometimes attempt.

There is no specific degree that leads to a job in quality assurance testing. This can make it a good starting position for someone with the right personality traits. However, one can get certification from the American Society for Quality, which teaches the fundamentals of quality testing and analysis for many different fields. It is also a good idea to study the recognized standards for quality that a company might use, such as Capability Model Maturity Integration, or CMMI.

Certification demonstrates that a person has knowledge of the best methods for testing and improving products. With certification and experience, a tester can potentially advance to becoming a quality assurance lead or a quality assurance manager. People in these positions oversee the process of testing, either for a specific product or for everything within the company, such as all company Web sites and applications.

REAL-TIME CUSTOMER SERVICE

Self-service forms of retail, such as online shopping, are great unless the customer has a problem or a question. In a regular store, customers look to employees who are expected to be able to help with customer concerns. Most online retailers have a readily activated e-mail link or an online form that customers can use to ask questions. However, responses can sometimes take a day or more.

To speed things up, retailers are enlisting the help of online customer service personnel. By clicking on an icon or link, customers can open a chat window to reach a live customer service agent who can help them. At the simplest level, online customer service representatives type back and forth with the customer until the issue is resolved. But most representatives can do more from their computer terminals than talk. In many cases, and with the customer's permission, the representative can view or control the customer's browser window so that both people can be on the same Web page.

To succeed in online customer service, people need to have good communication skills and the ability to type grammatically correct sentences rapidly and accurately. They should also know where frequently needed information can

Online customer service agents often work with customers by e-mail, online chat, and phone. Good communication and problem-solving skills are helpful in this job.

be found on the company's Web site. In some cases, knowing how to find and use customer account information is helpful. This might require some experience working with databases.

DATABASES: WAREHOUSES OF INFORMATION

Online retailers almost certainly use one or more databases in their normal operations. Databases are programs that hold large amounts of digital information to be retrieved as needed by individuals with proper access. Entries can be tagged or sorted into multiple categories for purposes of organization. Databases are where companies keep customer information and transaction histories, as well as inventories of products.

While there are several types of database software already in existence, some companies need to heavily modify existing software, or even create their own, to suit their specific needs. Whoever works heavily with a database should be a logical and analytic person who isn't intimidated by large amounts of information.

A database developer is a specialized software developer who can help a company create effective databases. In order to become database developers, people have to become familiar with SQL, the most common language for database construction. Many database developers go through certification in SQL and other database languages. They also need to learn how to organize, analyze, and troubleshoot problems with databases.

Often these skills are taught as part of a bachelor's degree program in management information systems (MIS), which is the preferred degree for database specialists. With experience and possibly a higher degree in business administration, a database developer could potentially become a database administrator who oversees a company's entire database system.

LOGISTICS

Maintaining inventory for a company that sells both online and at retail stores can be challenging. Companies want to

By recording levels of customer activity over time, logistics managers can better anticipate how to meet future demand.

have enough of their products on shelves that store customers can buy them, but not so many that there is no space to put them. They also need to have plenty of warehouse stock on hand to ship to online customers without making their stores short. The process of overseeing the supply chain that receives stock and ships it to stores and online customers is called logistics.

Logistics managers have to juggle a number of different business partner accounts, including those of suppliers, shipping companies, warehouses, and payment acquisition services such as PayPal. As a result, they have to be adept at working with lots of other companies' Web sites.

SUCCESS STORY: AKAMAI

The Internet's explosive success would not have been possible if getting information from it took a long time at each step. The convenience of shopping online would not exist if a customer had to wait a half hour between clicking on a link to look at some coats and getting to see them. However, in the late 1980s and early 1990s, the problem of finding and retrieving information quickly and easily was a huge threat to the Internet. The system that people now know as the World Wide Web was a large part of the solution. It helped organize, sort, and format information through graphic browsers, translating the data into things people could see and work with.

Although the invention of the World Wide Web improved matters, popular sites or ones that had sudden surges of interest could still be slowed down to the point of being unworkable due to heavy traffic. A group of mathematicians worked together in the 1990s to create a set of algorithms that could be used to order and prioritize data in order for it to travel faster. This system for quickly transmitting large amounts of data was one of the ultimate feats in network engineering and formed the foundation for a company, Akamai. Akamai, which means "intelligent" in Hawaiian, now licenses its systems to major online companies that do a lot of media streaming or have heavy Internet traffic. Apple, Facebook, and Netflix have all been Akamai customers at some point. The company's brilliant methods of data packet transfers became a business in itself that helped make online retail possible.

Decades of work on how networks transmit data—by Akamai and other companies—have enabled speedy loading of Web content today.

Since logistics managers are ultimately focused on making sure customers can easily get the things they want to buy, they have to be able to respond quickly. A frustrated customer, or one who cannot order something because it is out of stock, is potentially a lost customer. Until recently, an associate's degree in business was all that was necessary to become a logistics manager. Today, most companies look for people who have at least a bachelor's degree in logistics or business.

NETWORK ENGINEERS

While logistics deals with receiving and transporting packages in the real world, another job involves tracking the movement of packets in the digital realm. A lot of data flows into and out of an online retail company's Web site and data servers. If this information is not handled well, a Web site could get bogged down and crash, customer information and orders could get lost, and digital media might not stream or download. In order to keep information moving quickly and efficiently, companies hire data network engineers or network troubleshooters.

When data is moved from place to place over a network or across the Internet, it is broken down into smaller chunks. These chunks are sent across a network connection and reassembled on a receiving computer. How the data is broken down depends on network protocols, which are determined by the type of network connection. Network engineers study the information contained in these chunks, often called packets, to look for problems. Seeing how the tiny bits of data are organized can reveal flaws or mistakes to be corrected.

Packet analysis can be beneficial in many areas, including software development, and can be learned while pursuing a bachelor's degree in computer science. Company-wide data packet engineering is a highly advanced skill, often requiring a master's degree or even a doctorate in computer science. In fact, one of the largest online retailers, Amazon.com, sometimes calls its network engineers "data ninjas" because of the fine work and immense difficulty of the job.

CERTIFICATIONS

There are plenty of certifications available for database managers and network engineers. Nearly every form of network technology, such as Cisco routers and IBM Ethernet products, has a certification from its manufacturers. In many cases, employers require certification for the database software and network hardware they use. Since the technology continually changes, certification in these areas might expire quickly and require recertification, as often as once a year in some cases. Employers often pay for the recertification process.

CHAPTER 4

Technical Support

Computer technicians are a common and vital part of many businesses today. In online retail, having technical support is incredibly important. Having a company's Web site crash or servers go offline would be like having a brick-and-mortar store be closed or heavily damaged. No business could get done, nothing could get sold, and valuable data or digital products could get lost or stolen.

In addition, online retailers have to take great care in working on the Internet. Security for the customers—and for the company's data and profits—is the responsibility of the company. The bigger the company, the bigger a target it is for hackers and thieves. That's why online retailers need the best computer minds they can find.

ON-SITE COMPUTER TECHNICIANS

Even when an online retailer doesn't have a real-world storefront, it often has office buildings and on-site workers. Customer service personnel, business managers, and marketing professionals at these companies need the same level of technical help as people at other companies. Retailers that do business both in stores and online may have a large number of computers that need to be taken care of.

Whether it's a software driver problem or simply dead batteries in a cordless mouse, computer technicians and IT specialists must diagnose everyday computer problems quickly.

Computer technicians and information technology, or IT, specialists are the ones who make sure a company's computers stay operational. Some of the tasks they work on include upgrading software and hardware, troubleshooting problems with employees' computers, handling networking issues, dealing with troublesome printers, or simply unfreezing a frozen computer screen.

If a business's Web site is hosted on-site, computer technicians perform those same services for the server computers. They make sure the servers remain up and running, upgrade server software in a timely manner, and reboot servers quickly if they go offline. They might also monitor the servers for performance issues that could keep the servers from sending data to customers properly.

Real-world experience and enthusiasm may be all that is needed to get a first job as a computer technician. High school students who know their way around the inside of a computer and know how to solve common software problems might be able to get a job right out of high school. Strong candidates could probably build a computer from spare parts. They would know how to install operating system software and productivity software. They might already have been serving as a computer tech for friends and family who needed help in using their own computers. Basic computer enthusiasts might need to study up on working with servers, but knowing how to fix PCs is the number-one skill for this job.

DATA CENTER ENGINEER

In the same way that some businesses outsource their warehousing and shipping needs to another company with good facilities, many online retailers do the same thing for their data services. Colocation centers are warehouses that store, monitor, and service servers for many different clients. At a colocation center, stacked servers fill row upon row of racks within aggressively cooled rooms.

Data center engineers are responsible for making sure that these online businesses stay online. The engineers install backup servers so that Internet traffic can be switched over to another server if something goes wrong. They keep servers up-to-date with security software. They also connect the servers to fast data transmission sources for quick sending and receiving of information.

Understanding efficient data center structure is critical for data center engineers. Their knowledge goes beyond simple computer setup. For large centers, data center engineers must be able to design server architecture in a way that minimizes

In a data center, server racks like these might hold hundreds or thousands of individual servers capable of sending, receiving, and storing massive amounts of data.

wasted power. Colocation takes a lot of electricity, and if the server racks overload the power grid, hundreds or thousands of online retailers could go offline. Along with a computer science background, an electrical engineering degree can be helpful for this career. Data center engineers can also be certified as specialists in network security and server hardware through companies such as Cisco.

WEB AND DATA SECURITY

Online retail involves selling to customers using digital forms of payment. These include credit or debit cards, electronic bank transactions, and third-party payment services such as PayPal. Customers also supply personal information to online retailers such as full name, address, phone number, and other details. If outside parties were to get a hold of this data, they could create fake accounts or credit cards in a customer's name, make charges to another person's credit cards, or even steal money right out of a customer's bank account!

Security is of major importance to any trustworthy online retailer. Responsibility for Web security is put into the hands of data security analysts, engineers, and administrators. Data security analysts work on setting up security measures or testing them to find areas of improvement. A data security

A secure Web site is indicated by the Web address prefix "https" and often displays a lock icon to reassure customers.

engineer might design a means of data security for a company, possibly even writing unique software to help protect sensitive information. If a company is large enough or worried enough to have multiple people working on security, a data security administrator might be needed to coordinate all their efforts.

A small company's needs might include making sure all computers have up-to-date virus scan software and that the network has a firewall that can keep out unwanted connections. The bigger a company gets, however, the more attractive it becomes to hackers and criminals. In such cases, network security engineers or administrators monitor data traffic for unusual sources and types of data transfer. They set up safeguards on company databases to keep them from releasing information after computer commands are entered into online forms, an attack known as SQL injection. Often they secure their networks using encryption software so that even if data is stolen, it will still be protected with encryption.

Security also involves configuring servers and host machines to allow only wanted data to go in and out. By preventing a flood of nonsense data from bogging down the host computers, a data security engineer can keep hacker attacks from crashing a server or Web site.

Hackers develop new ways to attack computer systems all the time, so data security workers must remain up-to-date on the latest threats and the best defenses against them. Electronic transactions are an important area of concern for online retailers. During electronic transactions, the customer sends payment information to the retailer and the retailer confirms the payment and approves the customer's purchase. Hackers sometimes try to capture this data as it is transferring.

SOCIAL ENGINEERING

There's only so much data security workers can do for a company's computers and networks to keep it all secure. Even the best defenses are useless if a criminal can trick someone on the inside into leaving the virtual door open. Sometimes all a hacker needs is to get one or more e-mail addresses of people who work at a company. They can then send a fake e-mail pretending to be a relative, friend, or colleague at another company. If the criminal can get a person to visit a particular site, click on a link, or download and run a file, that criminal can take over the employee's computer without having to sneak through system protection.

Some forms of this social engineering, including phishing, do not involve computers at all until the end. The criminal might send targets fake mail or postcards stating that they could win a prize if they visit a particular Web site. Then when the target types in the Web address and follows the instructions, the hacker sends a virus or other malware onto the computer. As *SC Magazine* has reported, these attacks can be so sly that even the Pentagon has fallen prey to them a few times.

Any employees who have and use Internet access are potential targets, especially if they occasionally use computers for personal use, such as checking e-mail or shopping online. In a work environment where there are many employees with Internet access, a data security worker must be a good communicator. Data security workers need to inform other employees about these tricks so that they do not fall for them and make computer security useless.

The risk is high enough that banks and credit card companies require most retailers to follow a series of guidelines to protect transactions. Data security workers need to ensure that their company meets those standards in order to do business.

Depending on the company, an employer may require a credential from a bachelor's degree in information systems or computer science up to a doctorate. In addition, there are many certifications a data security worker might acquire, including secure software programming, exploit research, firewall analyst, and reverse-engineering malware.

CHIEF INFORMATION OFFICER

All of the technology departments in a company, from the Web development team to the network security team, report to the chief information officer (CIO). This individual sees that all of a retailer's computers and information systems work together and function as needed to help the company reach its goals. For example, the CIO makes sure that the inventory management software on the warehouse computers provides accurate data about whether an item is in stock. He or she works to keep customers' identities secure while still making sure that sales representatives can access the data to follow up with clients. In short, the CIO is in charge of a company's technology use and future needs.

Chief information officer is an executive-level position with high demands and responsibilities. A CIO must have a great deal of knowledge about the company's computer and network systems and software, while also being aware of alternative hardware or software solutions the company could be using. A CIO has to work within a company's budget to get the best equipment available that meets the requirements set by the chief executive officer, president, or company managers. Chief information officers often have a background in both computers and business and many years of experience

Few companies can afford to upgrade all their technology every year, so integrating computer systems that will be effective for many years is critical to a business. In larger companies, a CIO oversees such plans.

working in business information technology. A CIO is typically responsible for the personnel of various IT teams and might hire or fire workers to meet various needs.

Beyond running the day-to-day systems, a CIO has to plan for the future and know how a company will expand its technology in order to grow alongside the business. The CIO must make sure the company has the tools to continue doing business and to maintain and expand its customer base. In some cases, staying on the forefront of future technology is so important that this role might be split off into its own position, that of chief technology officer (CTO).

There are significant differences between getting potential customers to pay attention in the real world and getting them to pay attention on the Internet. A brand-new neighborhood store can attract looks while it's being built. Once finished, it can advertise in the local newspapers. The owners might buy commercial airtime on local radio stations or make commercials for local television stations. The surrounding community is easy to reach.

Online, customers could just as easily be local or from another country. This provides the opportunity for a larger customer pool, but it also makes it more difficult to grab the attention of customers from the surrounding community. Online retail marketing must be very aggressive to get potential customers to visit and purchase.

Online marketing also involves a high level of data analysis, as online retailers can monitor all activity on their sites. The interactivity of the Internet also lends itself to individualized marketing. Retailers can use information about a customer's location, devices, and online activity to target each user's specific interests. As a result, the best online marketers use a perfect balance of mathematical formulation and creative expression.

SEARCH ENGINE OPTIMIZATION MANAGER

A search engine is a bit like a phone book for the Internet. When people want to find information or shop for a product on the Internet, they often use a search engine to get recommendations for where to go on the Web. Search engines are so widely used that many people use a search engine as the starting page on their computer's Web browser. Most Web browsers have search entry lines on each browser page or a tab that users can use to search for something immediately instead of having to go to the search engine home page.

Search engine software, such as Microsoft's Bing search engine and Google's Web search, use automated processes to retrieve Web sites, archive text, follow the links on sites, and monitor traffic to Web addresses. Search engines organize or rank the pages so that users are more likely to get the results they want when they enter a search term. The more relevant the software determines a Web page to be with regard to a specific type of search, the higher it appears in the vertical list of results. Since most people will click on one of the first results they are shown, online retailers often use search engine optimization managers to help the retailer's Web site appear as high as possible in the results. Each engine uses its own formula for calculating which Web sites to recommend. Search engine optimization managers constantly try to crack that formula in order to increase their site's rank.

To boost results, search engine managers often use keywords, which are commonly used search terms or categories that apply to the retailer's goods or services. These keywords are included

Search engines such as Bing, Google, and Yahoo! process an enormous amount of data. Search engine optimization affects the visibility of a Web site in search results.

in a part of the Web page code that a search engine's automated processes will see, but most customers won't. If the retailer sells flashlights, the search engine optimization manager might add terms like "flashlight," "lantern," "camping," "glow-in-the-dark," "torch," and "battery-powered" to the HTML code for the pages about flashlights. He or she may even include misspellings, such as "flashlite," that people might use when searching. The right keywords will suggest to a search engine that the retailer's page is more relevant to the search than another site's page, and will cause the engine to list it higher.

As search engines become more capable of ignoring these hidden keywords, it is important for search engine managers to help write the text that displays on the page. Having good descriptions, titles, and content is even more effective at influencing page rankings than using keywords. Managers need to have strong language skills and knowledge about Web site layout and coding so that they can help design sites with easily accessible content. They also need to be able to interpret the retail site's logs to see what search terms are leading customers to the site. Then they can figure out how to build on those terms. Of course, search engine optimization managers must stay up-to-date on new information and changes in search engines' ranking formulas.

Working in search engine optimization is very much an experience-based job. Although there are certification courses in this field, the information can become outdated quickly as search engines improve and modify their search algorithms. Aspiring search engine managers would do best to combine real-world experience optimizing Web sites with a bachelor's degree in either computer science or marketing. Technologically capable English majors might have success in this area as well.

As optimization is a constantly changing process, many companies with a heavy Web presence hire interns to help monitor and fine-tune Web traffic. This can be a good way to get experience while still in school.

SOCIAL MEDIA REPRESENTATIVE

Retailers are very protective of their brand identity. Public relations, in which companies try to present a good "face" to all existing and potential customers, is critical online. From blogs to networking sites and message boards, there is no shortage of places where people can talk about their

COOKIES AND DATA TRACKERS

Online retailers and marketing specialists often use a controversial tech tool. When a customer's Web browser reaches the retailer's Web site, most retailers install a "cookie," which is a small bit of data containing information useful to the retailer. This cookie can contain login information, as well as other user-specific data. Some aggressive retailers set their cookie to track what other Web sites the customer visits. By learning what online interests and activities the customer spends time on, retailers can try to align their Web site's ads and displays to those interests. If they do it successfully, they can greatly increase the chances of making a sale. To a digital marketer, a well-created cookie can be a gold mine of data.

The downside is that some of these cookies invade a customer's privacy, especially if they seek out personal data or data about the customer's family. Cookies are also big targets for hackers, who hope to intercept or read the cookies to gain access to the customer's accounts or personal information. Most Web browsers allow customers to block or delete cookies at any time, but this can make some Web sites unusable. Internet users must constantly balance the need for privacy against the ease of using retail and other Web sites. Likewise, marketers and analysts for online retailers must decide for themselves how active and possibly intrusive a cookie will be in storing customer data.

experiences with a company. If that experience is negative, a retailer might look bad and even lose sales.

By using a social media representative, companies can extend their customer service beyond their retail Web site and energize loyal fans with frequent communications about new offers. While it helps if the social media representative is comfortable with Web technology and social media software, it is more important that he or she is a good communicator who is patient, able to relate to customers, and capable of writing well-formed sentences with proper spelling.

Whether it's on Facebook, Twitter, or a social outlet yet to be invented, a social media representative must be able to handle enthusiastic fans, angry critics, and everyone in between. Sometimes a representative even needs to calm down fights that erupt between those two extremes. Social media can be used simply to make announcements or offer deals. However, retailers make the strongest impact if they recognize that social media can be a dialogue with their customer base that doesn't involve constantly selling to them. Representatives must be thoughtful and levelheaded in their responses so that they do not express something that would misrepresent the company or bring bad publicity. At the same time, social media representatives can bring valid concerns and customer feedback to the appropriate persons within the company.

It's not uncommon for a retailer to have multiple representatives responsible for creating content and moderating interactions on social media. This is especially true when a retailer uses existing employees to make the posts and updates. When this is the case, all the involved employees need to be able to work well together to present a common voice to the public.

A job as a social media representative is a possibility for a young worker right out of high school or college who has deep experience working with social media. However, he or she would need to show a high level of maturity and professionalism in working with fellow employees and with customers online.

DATA ANALYST

One of the benefits of online retailing is the ability to track results and data in real time. In addition to sales and profit, Web tools and analysis software can tell such things as which products people often buy together, how much inventory should be kept on hand to meet sales, and which outside Web sites drive the most traffic to the company's Web site. Analysts can use that data to improve their sales strategies.

Data analysts for online retailers often have backgrounds in mathematics, statistics, economics, or business, perhaps in addition to computer science. They need to be logical and good with numbers, as well as competent communicators so that they can explain to others what the numbers mean. A well-rounded data analyst has the precision to accurately process results but also the creativity and insight to see connections between data sets. Since most of the data online retailers analyze comes from either the company's databases or Web tracking software, data analysts need to be comfortable working within databases or with Web site tools. They may even want to become certified in those areas.

Some online retailers hire data analysts on a short-term basis to analyze a specific set of data. For instance, a store that offered a special promotion both online and in-store might need someone to measure the success of the promotions so as to maximize future efforts. Using freelance analysts or analysts from an independent company can give the retailer a neutral analysis. Freelancers have the chance to solve new problems in new environments, which is appealing to analysts who love a challenge.

Data analysts can work in nearly every segment of online retail, from assessing customer service results to monitoring warehouse inventory. Some data analysts even become project managers because their data can help establish and measure metrics, or means of measuring success, for branches of the company.

DIGITAL ADVERTISING OR MARKETING MANAGER

Armed with loads of customer data and Web site statistics, a digital advertising manager determines the best strategy for advertising that will bring traffic to a retail Web site. By tracking existing customers' activities, digital advertisers find out how people get directed to their Web sites. If many customers are following a link from a specific external site that leads to the retail Web site, the digital advertising manager might consider buying advertisements to run on that Web site. If the retailer already advertises there, the digital manager might purchase more or bigger ads to catch even more traffic. The digital advertising manager or digital marketer's job is to get more customers to visit the Web site, which would hopefully translate to more sales.

Marketing for an online retailer often involves a healthy amount of real-world marketing. Even online-only retailers use traditional advertising channels such as print magazine ads or television commercials. However, while both online and

With so many people going online, Web marketing is important for drawing customers to a company or brand. Success for a Web marketing manager often means reaching a target number of new visitors to a site.

real-world ads try to lure consumers to shop, online advertising is unique in that it is possible to track the exact numbers of views and level of success of an advertisement. For example, if short messages on a social media service regularly generate more traffic than another method, such as an e-mail blast, the manager might decide to invest more time attracting customers through social media. However, the best marketers are able to recognize short-term trends but also hold on to the big picture. The ability to think long-term keeps marketers from overreacting to occasional shifts in the market.

Since online marketing is an extension of traditional marketing, a marketing background is important in this

SUCCESS STORY: GOOGLE ANALYTICS AND ADWORDS

Early online retailers needed the help of their information technology departments to find out how many customers were visiting a site and what they were doing there. IT staff had to pore over the server logs and analyze the data. It was a long and difficult process, and it often took up time needed to work on other things. In 1998, a company called Urchin Software began selling an alternative method. Retailers could pay Urchin Software to analyze the data for them. All they needed to do was add some code to their Web pages that would send user information to Urchin.

The product was so successful that in 2005, Google bought the company and its technology and created Google Analytics. Google combined Urchin's software with the technology behind its Web search software to provide an efficient way for companies to use data from customer visits. The offer of free analysis was so popular that Google had to make the service invitation-only for years. Eventually, Google decided to offer a standard version of the service for free and then charge a subscription fee for premium service.

Google's moneymaking truly took off when it launched AdWords, a service that allowed retailers to purchase text ads that appeared alongside search results. Retailers purchased ads that would activate when people used search terms or phrases that related to the retailer's goods or services. By offering its search engine and standard analytics service for free, Google was able to sell an additional service that could effectively find potential customers. Thanks in large part to AdWords, Google reported over $36 billion of revenue in 2011 on its investor relations Web page.

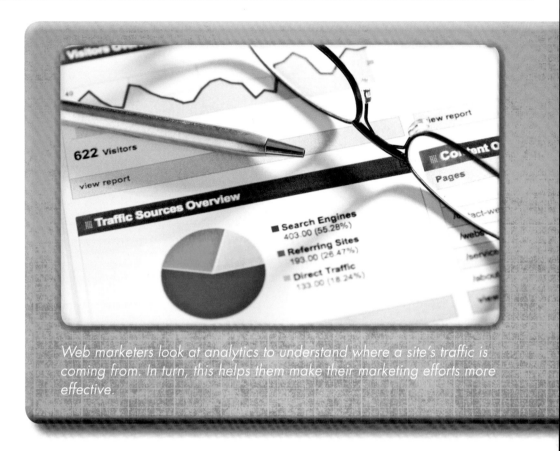

Web marketers look at analytics to understand where a site's traffic is coming from. In turn, this helps them make their marketing efforts more effective.

field. A college degree in marketing, communications, business, psychology, or sociology is helpful. Marketers with a strong interest and understanding of computers and the Internet can be effective digital marketing managers even without a degree in computer science or software certification. However, experienced online marketers need to know how to use mass mailing programs or services, analytics programs for tracking customer response, and popular social media services.

CONVERSION OPTIMIZATION SPECIALISTS

While marketers focus on bringing more and more potential customers to the Web site or retail service, another kind of specialist focuses on turning more of those visits into sales. The term for turning visits into sales is "conversion." Marketers or businesspeople with a lot of experience working with and selling to online customers might become adept at increasing conversion rates. If they are really good at it, they might become conversion optimization specialists.

Conversion optimization involves looking at the entire business from the customer's point of view. In many cases, systems may be working properly but not effectively. Perhaps the online shopping cart is too confusing to use with discount codes. Maybe it is too difficult to compare similar brands or models on the Web site. The specialist might find that people have trouble remembering or spelling the Web site's name. Anything that causes customers to give up on using or buying from the retailer is a threat to conversion.

It's not unusual for a conversion optimization specialist to oversee large, sweeping changes and new programs to a retail business. For the already popular BabyAge.com, a conversion-optimization consulting group was able to further increase the company's sales of baby-related items. By testing different variations of the site's welcome page and item-description pages, the consultants created a layout that led to more customer purchases. The combination of visual appeal and ease of use led to a more than 20 percent increase in the site's conversion rate.

CHAPTER 6

Digital Distribution Retailers

A long with the usual retail process of buying, selling, and shipping products, there are a number of forms of retail that can only be e-commerce. These opportunities fall into the category of content creation. Many forms of media and entertainment are available for use on computers or smartphones, either in addition to a real-world product or all by themselves. Creative and hardworking people who have computer skills and other talents can combine those interests to make money online.

DIGITAL VERSIONS OF PRINT MEDIA

More and more people get their news from the Internet because they can learn about events minutes after they happen. Meanwhile, it can take half a day for newspapers and a week or more for magazines to cover newsworthy events. Many newspapers and print magazines have Web sites where breaking news can be shared quickly and then examined more closely in a longer article later. The full article may appear in both print and online form, either for free or through a paid subscription. Often additional material not found in the print publication is available online. The newsmagazine *Time*, for instance, has additional content for its print subscribers to access online.

The Web sites of newspapers and magazines work on balancing the presentation of longer, in-depth stories with the customer's desire for quick snippets or summaries of information.

As a result, many print publications need content editors for their Web sites or apps. A digital content editor takes the text and images for submitted stories and adds them to the Web site to keep the site up-to-date. He or she might also archive old stories on the site for reference.

An editor or writer who is comfortable with layout and basic programming for Web sites is a great fit for this position, which requires attention to detail and thoroughness. All the text and images need to appear in the right places, as well as flow and link properly with other parts of the site.

DIGITAL PHOTOGRAPHY

The Internet can serve as an excellent art gallery. Just as most print publications have turned to digital layout, they have also turned toward digital images. Photographers using digital cameras who are also good with photo-editing software and Web design can showcase their afternoon's work to the Internet that same evening. With digital stock photography and individual artist Web sites, potential customers can quickly find the images they need for a variety of uses. Most digital artists "tag" their photos and images with search terms a person might use to look for such images, making them easier to find.

One problem with selling digital images is that it is relatively easy for people to copy and reuse images without permission. However, computer-savvy digital artists usually create safeguards such as digital watermarks over the image and displaying low-resolution or incomplete images in their online galleries.

With some knowledge of HTML, CSS, and Flash, in addition to whatever software they use for their art, digital

Unless online images are clearly labeled as free for use, people must get permission or pay for rights in order to use them. Photographers need to do their research in order to get the best fees for their work.

artists have the ability to make and sell stunning works of art. Interactive art might even move or respond to the viewer's mouse clicks and motions. Web comic artists, motion comic artists, and virtual sculptors have all found success working and selling mostly online.

E-BOOK PUBLISHING

Digital readers such as Amazon's Kindle and the Barnes & Noble Nook have grown enough in popularity that many traditional publishers have begun selling electronic copies of their books. At first, e-books looked much like word-processing documents with the text of the book flowing from page to page. The PDF, or portable document format, has been another popular way of publishing digital books, allowing the publisher to set images and text as it wished. With EPUB, the International Digital Publishing Forum created a free means of formatting data for e-books. The organization reported that EPUB allowed vendors to sell over $400 million in digital publishing in 2010.

While the first phases of e-book publishing consisted of traditional publishers moving to digital technology, computer technology enthusiasts have begun establishing their own visions of what e-book publishing and retailing can be like. Today, there is a market for well-written, self-published e-books. Anyone skilled in working with EPUB, PDFs, or device-specific formats can create them. So long as they meet the required standards for Amazon's e-book listings, independently created e-books can be listed on the retail giant's Web site alongside those from traditional publishers. There are, in fact, many companies whose business is to help customers convert their texts into e-books for either personal or commercial use. By learning how to properly

ONLINE CURRENCY

The interconnectedness of online retail has given rise to new and expanded international markets. It has also seen the creation of its own forms of currency, with real-world exchange rates. For example, Blizzard's online games *World of Warcraft* and *Diablo 3* are used by so many dedicated players that it is possible to sell in-game gold and items for real-world money.

One example comes from perhaps the most popular social network in the world. As Facebook prepared to become a publicly held company, it needed to find new ways to make the free site profitable. Besides running Web ads, the company rolled out Facebook Credits. This virtual currency could be purchased and used in the entertainment apps on the site that offered premium content. The "freemium" model, in which customers can play for free but need to purchase gold or tokens to excel, has become a standard for online entertainment.

Another experiment in online commerce is the artificially created currency called bitcoins. Bitcoins are generated by large groups of computers that devote their processors to solving complex problems. The ownership of all existing bitcoins is saved in a network shared by users of the bitcoin program. Bitcoin users believe that this currency is more secure and more stable than other types of currency, and because no banks are involved, fees are small or nonexistent.

format text for e-readers, individuals and companies can profit not just from selling their own e-books but also from providing the service to other authors without those skills.

One way to begin learning is to work directly with the software recommended by a particular sales platform, such as

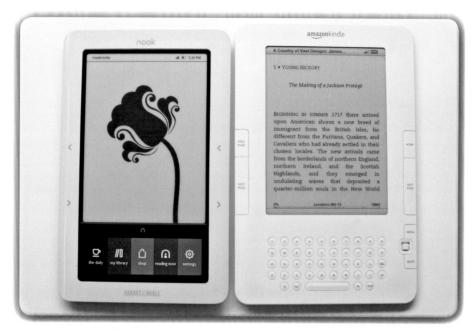

E-readers are among the 425 million Internet-capable devices in the United States today. All of these devices create markets for new content.

Apple's iBooks Author program. A programmer could even write his or her own app that allows people to make and share e-books themselves.

WEB VIDEO

Today, high-speed Internet access has become the norm, enabling quick downloads and even streaming of top-quality video and audio. Companies such as Netflix, Hulu, Apple, and Amazon pose a serious challenge to cable and satellite programming providers. By offering access to on-demand

SUCCESS STORY: ROOSTER TEETH PRODUCTIONS

One of the most wildly successful online Web series of all time started with a trio of tech support workers who enjoyed video games. Shortly after the game *Halo* was released in 2001, tech workers Burnie Burns, Geoff Fink, and Gustavo Sorola began staging scenes in the game, a technique called machinima. They recorded these scenes and their own voice tracks to create a series of Web videos they called *Red vs. Blue*, referring to the multiplayer mode of that game.

The group posted their videos on the Internet, where *Halo* fans and other gaming fans made them some of the most downloaded videos on the Web. It wasn't long before the team, calling itself Rooster Teeth, grew in size and began creating full seasons of episodes, varying in length from about six to twelve minutes each. These videos were eventually combined and sold as DVDs, helping to fund further efforts.

As additional versions of the *Halo* game were made, the tools the team used became better and better as well. The production improved and the fan base grew. According to Rooster Teeth's YouTube channel, by 2012, the company's videos had been played over one billion times. The *Red vs. Blue* series proved so popular that the makers of the game built and shared custom assets within the game so that others could help them make their videos. Rooster Teeth even managed to attract high-end talent to their projects, including legendary machinima animator Monty Oum and movie actor Elijah Wood.

The company has a standard retail model, selling clothing and collections of its videos on DVD. It also uses a free mobile app that lets fans view videos and purchase items. However, the primary form of revenue comes from paid subscribers, who pay Rooster Teeth in order to have access to higher-quality video and the ability to stream or download the videos before the rest of the public.

viewing, companies can create a service model of retail limited only by the quality of programming offered.

Computer technicians are critical to this growing field. Digital video specialists must be able to edit video and optimize it for streaming. Localization experts are helpful, especially if they are bilingual, in preparing video to be viewed around the world. They use software such as Passolo and Catalyst to create captions, subtitles, and translations to accompany the video. Compressionists are specialists who focus on reducing the size of the data files without reducing the quality of the video too much. Audio engineers work to digitally record, clean, and compress sound. Many of these jobs are needed even if the production

The DVD-by-mail company Netflix has expanded into a digital streaming giant for movies and television. Computer specialists are needed at Netflix and other companies to provide consumers with high-quality video online.

simply involves taking existing analog video and converting it to digital. All of this is in addition to the software and hardware knowledge needed to create animations, special effects, title sequences, and other computerized elements already common in many forms of visual media.

INDEPENDENT SOFTWARE CREATORS

In the end, a computer enthusiast may simply choose to avoid a company setting and work alone. Programmers and code writers can become independent software creators and sell their software through marketplaces like the iTunes App Store, Xbox Live Indie Games, or c|net. In addition, programmers might choose to sell software through their own sites. With consumers' computers constantly connected to the Internet, it is easy to create demo versions that can be unlocked through an online purchase or access code. In this way, a person can profit from his or her programs directly instead of merging the work with an entire company's output.

Whether it's to boost one's résumé, bring in extra income, work full-time as an independent contractor, or bridge the gap between jobs, the Internet makes it possible for independent operators to sell and distribute their own software. The next big app that companies need, buy, and install may very well be created by one of the many programmers working at home with the freedom to choose how they want to apply their talents.

algorithm A sequence of instructions that, when followed in order, will resolve a particular problem.

broadband An Internet connection allowing for fast data transfers.

browser A computer program that allows users to view Web pages on the Internet.

certification The state of having demonstrated mastery of a particular set of professional skills, often resulting in the receipt of a certificate.

content The information that is stored on a Web site and that is accessible to standard users.

developer A person who writes computer code to meet specific requirements.

firewall A system that prevents unauthorized access to a computer network in order to maintain security, for example, by allowing only preapproved packets of data to pass through.

font A complete set of letters, numbers, and additional print characters created in a consistent style of form and size.

freelancer An independent worker hired to do work for a set, temporary term.

hacker A person who circumvents a security design and gains unauthorized access to a computer system.

hypertext Electronic text that can be read nonlinearly by following links within the text to a new location.

interface The connection between two systems that allows them to share information, such as between a user and a computer program.

plug-in A sub-program that adds functionality to an application.

programming The process of creating instructions for a computer to follow.

proprietary Legally belonging to a specific owner and protected from unauthorized use.

protocol A standard way of treating, formatting, and passing data in an electronic communications system.

retailing The activities involved in selling goods to consumers for personal use.

server A computer that provides services and centralized resources to client computers that make a connection to it.

smartphone A cellular phone that offers advanced capabilities similar to those of a personal computer.

traffic The measurement of the number of users that visit a Web site; the load on an electronic communications system.

transaction An exchange of goods, services, or funds.

For More Information

AIESEC United States
11 Hanover Square, Suite 1700
New York, NY 10005
(212) 757-3774
Web site: http://www.aiesecus.org
AIESEC is the largest youth-run organization in the world. It
helps students find international internships in a number
of fields, including information technology, to train them
to work in a global market.

American Institute for Graphic Artists (AIGA)
164 Fifth Avenue
New York, NY 10010
(212) 807-1990
Web site: http://www.aiga.org
The AIGA, which has local chapters in nearly every state, is
committed to advancing design as a professional craft
and vital cultural force. There are resources available for
student and professional members on topics such as Web
design, interaction design, and user response to design
elements.

Association for Computing Machinery (ACM)
2 Penn Plaza, Suite 701
New York, NY 10121-0701
(212) 869-7440
Web site: http://www.acm.org
This organization shares resources to help further

computing as both a scientific and a social force. It connects employers with qualified candidates and offers information about computing careers. Special interest groups within the organization focus on specific aspects of computing, such as electronic commerce and human-computer interaction.

International Webmasters Association (IWA)
119 East Union Street, Suite #F
Pasadena, CA 91103
(626) 449-3709
Web site: http://www.iwanet.org
The IWA exists to advance the skills of Web designers and help them advance in their careers. The organization offers certification and programming coursework online, as well as networking for Web professionals.

MIT Center for Digital Business
5 Cambridge Center—NE25
Cambridge, MA 02142
(617) 253-7054
Web site: http://ebusiness.mit.edu
The MIT Center for Digital Business is the world's largest center for research focused on the digital economy. Its research projects investigate the latest trends and techniques in digital business.

Retail Council of Canada (RCC)
1255 Bay Street, Suite 800
Toronto, ON M5R 2A9
Canada

(888) 373-8245

Web site: http://www.retailcouncil.org

The Retail Council of Canada is an advocacy group for
retailers in Canada. The organization's education arm,
the Canadian Retail Institute (CRI), focuses on education, certification, and scholarship programs for students
interested in retail as a profession.

Software & Information Industry Association (SIIA)

1090 Vermont Avenue NW, 6th Floor

Washington, DC 20005-4095

(202) 289-7442

Web site: http://www.siia.net

The SIIA provides resources and learning opportunities for
professionals in the software and digital content industry.
It offers helpful information for businesses that deal with
digital distribution of their products.

WEB SITES

Due to the changing nature of Internet links, Rosen Publishing
has developed an online list of Web sites related to the subject
of this book. This site is updated regularly. Please use this link
to access the list:

http://www.rosenlinks.com/CICT/Retail

Berger, Lauren. *All Work, No Pay: Finding an Internship, Building Your Resume, Making Connections, and Gaining Job Experience.* Berkeley, CA: Ten Speed Press, 2012.

Collier, Marsha. *The Ultimate Online Customer Service Guide: How to Connect with Your Customers to Sell More!* Hoboken, NJ: Wiley, 2011.

Conway, Joe, and Aaron Hillegass. *iOS Programming: The Big Nerd Ranch Guide.* 3rd ed. Atlanta, GA: Big Nerd Ranch, 2012.

Ford, Jerry Lee. *Scratch Programming for Teens.* Boston, MA: Course Technology, 2009.

Fox, Vanessa. *Marketing in the Age of Google: Your Online Strategy Is Your Business Strategy.* Rev. ed. Hoboken, NJ: Wiley, 2012.

Frain, Ben. *Responsive Web Design with HTML5 and CSS3.* Birmingham, England: Packt Publishing, Ltd., 2012.

Funk, Tom. *Web 2.0 and Beyond: Understanding the New Online Business Models, Trends, and Technologies.* Westport, CT: Praeger, 2009.

Johnson, Jeff. *Designing with the Mind in Mind: Simple Guide to Understanding User Interface Design Rules.* Boston, MA: Morgan Kaufmann Publishers/Elsevier, 2010.

Joshi, Girdhar. *Information Technology for Retail* (Oxford Higher Education). New York, NY: Oxford University Press, 2009.

Kalbach, James. *Designing Web Navigation.* Sebastopol, CA: O'Reilly, 2007.

McDowell, Gayle Laakman. *Cracking the Coding Interview: 150 Programming Interview Questions and Solutions.* 5th ed. Palo Alto, CA: CareerCup, LLC, 2011.

McFarland, David Sawyer. *JavaScript & jQuery: The Missing Manual.* 2nd ed. Sebastopol, CA: O'Reilly, 2012.

Stallings, William. *Network Security Essentials: Applications and Standards.* 4th ed. Boston, MA: Pearson, 2011.

Tittel, Ed, and Jeff Noble. *HTML, xHTML & CSS for Dummies.* 7th ed. Hoboken, NJ: Wiley, 2011.

Wigdor, Daniel, and Dennis Wixon. *Brave NUI World: Designing Natural User Interfaces for Touch and Gesture.* Burlington, MA: Morgan Kaufmann, 2011.

Bibliography

Amazon Careers. "Careers Center—Position Details—CloudFront and Route 53 Data Ninja." August 24, 2012. Retrieved June 21, 2012 (https://us-amazon.icims.com/jobs/174045/job).

Bureau of Labor Statistics, U.S. Department of Labor. "Computer and Information Systems Managers." *Occupational Outlook Handbook*, 2012–13 Edition. Retrieved July 10, 2012 (http://www.bls.gov.

Bureau of Labor Statistics, U.S. Department of Labor. "Information Security Analysts, Web Developers, and Computer Network Architects." *Occupational Outlook Handbook*, 2012–13 Edition. Retrieved June 30, 2012 (http://www.bls.gov.

Burns, Daniel M. "The History of Google AdWords." Ezine Articles.com, June 9, 2010. Retrieved July 15, 2012 (http://ezinearticles.com/?The-History-of-Google-AdWords&id=4448970).

CareerBuilder.com. "Working as a Chief Information Officer." April 4, 2012. Retrieved July 30, 2012 (http://www.career builder.com/Article/CB-2992-IT-Working-as-a-chief-information-officer).

Dusto, Amy. "Fickle Friends: Detailed Analytics Help Web Retailers Solve the Value Puzzle of Social Shoppers." InternetRetailer.com, August 1, 2012. Retrieved August 2, 2012 (http://www.internetretailer.com/2012/08/01/fickle-friends).

Eberts, Marjorie, and Margaret Gisler. *Careers for Computer Buffs & Other Technological Types*. 3rd ed. New York, NY: McGraw Hill, 2006.

Farr, J. Michael. *Top 100 Computer and Technical Careers: Your Complete Guidebook to Major Jobs in Many Fields at All Training Levels* (JIST's Top Careers). 3rd ed. Indianapolis, IN: JIST Works, 2007.

Goldberg, Jan, and Mark Rowh. *Great Jobs for Computer Science Majors.* 2nd ed. Chicago, IL: VGM Career Books, 2003.

Heller, Laura. "The Future of Online Shopping: 10 Trends to Watch." Forbes.com, April 20, 2011. Retrieved June 28, 2012 (http://www.forbes.com/sites/lauraheller/2011/04/20/the-future-of-online-shopping-10-trends-to-watch).

History.com. "The Death Spiral of Napster Begins—This Day in History—3/6/2001." Retrieved July 3, 2012 (http://www.history.com/this-day-in-history/the-death-spiral-of-napster-begins).

Leiner, Barry M., et al. "Brief History of the Internet." Internet Society. Retrieved June 20, 2012 (http://www.internet society.org/internet/internet-51/history-internet/brief-history-internet).

Liberty, Jesse. *The Complete Idiot's Guide to a Career in Computer Programming.* Indianapolis, IN: Que, 1999.

Martinez, Anne. *Get Certified and Get Ahead.* New York, NY: McGraw-Hill, 1998.

Matti, Kirsten. Interview with the author. August 25, 2012.

Meyer, Robinson. "Stanford's Top Major Is Now Computer Science." *The Atlantic,* June 29, 2012. Retrieved July 1, 2012 (http://finance.yahoo.com/news/stanfords-top-major-now-computer-162724708.html).

Moscaritolo, Angela. "Pentagon Official Reveals 'Most Significant' Military Breach." *SC Magazine,* August 26, 2010. Retrieved November 30, 2012 (http://www.scmagazine

.com/pentagon-official-reveals-most-significant-military-breach/article/177586).

Nielson Company. "Panel Discussion: The Future of Online Retailing." *Nielsen Wire*, June 21, 2011. Retrieved June 28, 2012 (http://blog.nielsen.com/nielsenwire/consumer/panel-discussion-the-future-of-online-retailing).

Pearson, Mia. "Social Media Plays Growing Role in Online Retailing." *The Globe and Mail*, May 17, 2012. Retrieved June 27, 2012 (http://www.theglobeandmail.com).

U.S. Census Bureau. "Table 1055. Retail Trade Sales—Total and E-commerce by Kind of Business: 2009." *Statistical Abstract of the United States: 2012*. Retrieved June 27, 2012 (http://www.census.gov/compendia/statab/cats/wholesale_retail_trade/online_retail_sales.html).

U.S. Census Bureau. "Table 1056. Electronic Shopping and Mail-Order Houses—Total and E-Commerce Sales by Merchandise Line." *Statistical Abstract of the United States: 2012*. Retrieved June 27, 2012 (http://www.census.gov/compendia/statab/cats/wholesale_retail_trade/online_retail_sales.html).

Webb, Geoff. "The Evolution of Malware and Information Security." eSecurity Planet, May 25, 2011. Retrieved July 3, 2012 (http://www.esecurityplanet.com/trends/article.php/3934496/The-Evolution-of-Malware-and-Information-Security.htm).

WetFeet.com. *Careers in Information Technology* (WetFeet Insider Guide). San Francisco, CA: WetFeet, 2006.

Index

ABOUT THE AUTHOR

Jason Glaser is the author of over sixty fiction and nonfiction books for all ages. He taught himself HTML and Web site creation in the mid-1990s while earning his English degree at Augustana College in Sioux Falls, South Dakota. He has Microsoft certification in business and database software, and has served as the technology coordinator for Grace Lutheran Church in Mankato, Minnesota, since 2008.

PHOTO CREDITS

Cover (background), p. 1 © iStockphoto.com/Andrey Prokhorov; front cover (inset) Alejandro Rivera/E+/Getty Images; p. 5 Caroline Purser/Photographer's Choice/Getty Images; p. 9 ColorBlind Images/Iconica/Getty Images; pp. 11, 31 iStockphoto/Thinkstock; p. 13 Valeriy Lebedev/Shutterstock.com; p. 16 Izabela Habur/E+/Getty Images; p. 20 age fotostock/SuperStock; p. 22 Chris Gramly/the Agency Collection/Getty Images; p. 26 David McNew/Getty Images; pp. 29, 35 © AP Images; p. 33 Morgan Lane Photography/Shutterstock.com; p. 39 Edw/Shutterstock.com; p. 41 Baran Özdemir/Vetta/Getty Images; p. 42 © iStockphoto.com/Günay Mutlu; p. 46 Ryan McVay/Digital Vision/Getty Images; p. 49 © iStockphoto.com/serts; p. 55 Jupiterimages/Pixland/Thinkstock; p. 57 Oxford/E+/Getty Images; p. 60 © iStockphoto.com/ugurhan; p. 61 Courtesy of LVA Studios; p. 64 Bloomberg/Getty Images; p. 66 Gareth Cattermole/Getty Images; interior page border image © iStockphoto.com/Daniel Brunner; pp. 10, 15, 21, 25, 34, 35, 44, 51, 56, 57, 63, 65 (text box background) © iStockphoto.com/Nicholas Belton.

Designer: Matt Cauli; Editor: Andrea Sclarow Paskoff; Photo Editor: Karen Huang